Pennsylvania Lumber Museum

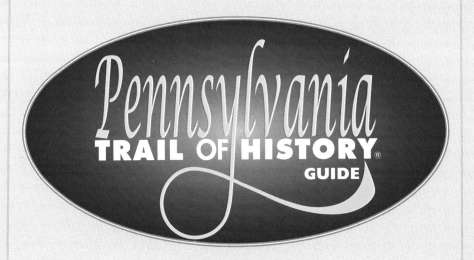

Text by Robert Currin

STACKPOLE BOOKS

PENNSYLVANIA HISTORICAL
AND MUSEUM COMMISSION

Kyle R. Weaver, Series Editor
Tracy Patterson, Designer

Published by
STACKPOLE BOOKS
5067 Ritter Road
Mechanicsburg, Pennsylvania 17055

Pennsylvania Trail of History® is a registered trademark of the Pennsylvania Historical and Museum Commission.

Printed in the United States of America
2 4 6 8 10 9 7 5 3 1
FIRST EDITION

Maps by Caroline Stover

Cover: Saw Mill and Log Holding Pond at the site.
CURT WEINHOLD
Page 3: Haskin's Camp in the hemlock forest near the East Fork
of the Susquehanna River, circa 1903.
PENNSYLVANIA LUMBER MUSEUM
Page 5: Unloading bark at a tannery.
PENNSYLVANIA LUMBER MUSEUM

Library of Congress Cataloging-in-Publication Data

Currin, Robert.
 Pennsylvania Lumber Museum : Pennsylvania trail of history guide / text by Robert Currin ; photographs by Art Becker.— 1st ed.
  p. cm. — (Pennsylvania trail of history guides)
 Includes bibliographical references.
 ISBN 0-8117-2965-6
 1. Pennsylvania Lumber Museum—Guidebooks. 2. Lumber trade—Pennsylvania—History. I. Becker, Art. II. Pennsylvania Historical and Museum Commission. III. Pennsylvania Lumber Museum. IV. Title. V. Series.

HD9757.P4C87 2005
634.9'8'074748—dc22

2004026124

Contents

Editor's Preface
4

Introduction to the Site
5

Pennsylvania's Forests
7

The Lumber Industry in Pennsylvania
13

Visiting the Site
40

Further Reading
48

Editor's Preface

With its vast abundance of natural resources, Pennsylvania became a leader in several industries during the nineteenth and early-twentieth centuries—anthracite coal mining, iron and steel manufacturing, railroading, and lumbering. The Pennsylvania Historical and Museum Commission (PHMC) has preserved the heritage of these industries in several museums that it administers throughout the state. This volume focuses on the Pennsylvania Lumber Museum, and with its publication Stackpole Books is pleased to continue its collaboration with the PHMC on the Pennsylvania Trail of History Guides series.

Each volume in the series features one of the historic sites or museums administered by the PHMC. The series was conceived and created by Stackpole Books with the cooperation of the PHMC's Division of Publications and Bureau of Historic Sites and Museums. Donna Williams heads the latter, and she and her staff of professionals review the text of each guidebook for accuracy and have made many valuable recommendations. Diane Reed, Chief of Publications, has facilitated relations between the PHMC and Stackpole from the project's inception, organized the review process with the commission, and attended to numerous details related to the venture. The first people at the commission I spoke to in 1998, when I originally developed the idea for a series of Trail of History guidebooks, were site administrators Michael Ripton, formerly of Ephrata Cloister; Douglas A. Miller, of Pennsbury Manor; and James A. Lewars, of Daniel Boone Homestead. The guidance and encouragement these gentlemen offered me led to discussions with the PHMC and the launching of the project.

For this volume, Dolores Buchsen, Administrator of the Pennsylvania Lumber Museum, went to great lengths to ensure that every detail was correct and was so committed to the project that she dashed out on one snowy winter day to deliver archival photos to me on time. Trisha Berberich, Records Manager, assisted with the photo research. Art Becker, whose work has appeared in several other volumes in this series, supplemented the book with photographs of the Bark Peelers' Convention and the site today. At Stackpole, David Reisch assisted me on production.

Robert Currin, author of the text, is a former teacher and currently curator of the Potter County Historical Society. He has written numerous articles on early lumbering, and here he offers a survey of the industry in Pennsylvania, background on operations in the north-central part of the state, and a tour of the museum grounds.

Kyle R. Weaver, Editor
Stackpole Books

Introduction to the Site

The Pennsylvania Lumber Museum, located on 160 timbered acres in north-central Pennsylvania's Potter County, tells the story of the harvesting and renewal of one of the commonwealth's most important resources. It shows how the use of lumber increased until the forests were completely harvested and how the renewable trees grew to provide another harvest.

The museum exhibits show the life and work of lumbermen during the successive eras when rivers, railroads, and trucks were used to transport timber to the mills and the lumber to the markets. Each story is different, but each era contributed to the commonwealth's rich lumbering heritage. The museum exhibits the equipment that at one time led Pennsylvania to become the leading lumber producer in the nation. One of the museum's primary missions is to show how the sustainable forests will be used in the future.

Pennsylvania's Forests

Except for the soil itself, no part of the environment has played a more important role in the development of the Commonwealth of Pennsylvania than its forests. From the beginning, great pressure was put on the vegetation of the virgin forests. The first farmers removed it to make way for needed cropland, but within a few years, the resource itself was put to use.

The early agrarian pioneers were not able to develop the land without first harvesting the trees that covered more than 90 percent of the area. As settlers moved to the piedmont, valleys, mountains, and plateaus, trees presented either a barrier that had to be removed or a source of wealth to be extracted.

As the nation's population increased and Philadelphia developed into its largest urban area, Pennsylvania's forests became the source of supply for industry. Settlement moved toward the interior of the country, putting more pressure on the forest industry to supply the materials for a wide variety of products, including tools, firearms, furniture, fuel, toys, firkins, dyes, and even medicine. For more than two hundred years, Penn's Woods provided virgin timber to meet the demands of civilization, until that timber eventually was used up. Today the offspring of the early forest continues in its place, supplying wood products to the nation.

EARLY SETTLEMENT

The Swedes, Dutch, and English who moved into the lower Delaware Valley during the mid-seventeenth century were awed by the forests. They had seen nothing in Europe to compare with the giant white pine, hemlock, maple, and oak trees that stood in their way.

As the settlers cleared land for the plow, some of the felled trees were used to construct log cabins. But there were too few settlers to use all of the harvested timber, so they piled up the excess logs and burned them. The need for lumber increased as more people arrived, and fewer trees were wasted. William Penn was among the first to recognize timber as a valuable resource and put restrictions on cutting, instructing "that in clearing ground, care be taken to leave

Pine Forest. The state's forests shaped its history for generations and produced a booming industry that for a time provided lumber for much of the nation. CURT WEINHOLD

one acre of trees for every five cleared; especially to preserve oak and mulberries for silk and shipping." When John Printz formed the Swedish colony at Tinicum in 1643, he was instructed to look at the forests as a source of wealth from which to cull choice woods.

As southeastern Pennsylvania gained in population and the number of wood workers increased, the nearby forests were rapidly cleared. This created a problem that the timber industry faced for many years: how to get the logs and lumber products to market. Because wood floats, the region's merchants began to use waterways for the transportation of logs. Two Pennsylvania rivers that reached into the interior forest lands, the Delaware and Susquehanna, were nearby. Both of these became major highways and remained so for more than two hundred years. Later the Allegheny and its tributaries became the highway to serve the western metropolis of Pittsburgh. Many logs shipped on that river reached New Orleans, at the mouth of the Mississippi River. These rivers and their tributaries were declared public highways and remain so today.

By the time of the American Revolution, Philadelphia was the largest city in the British colonies. Few ports could compete with its business in wood and wood products. Before the Revolutionary War, many settlers had moved toward the headwaters of the Susquehanna, but the Native Americans forced those along the West Branch to flee. The settlers returned near the end of the war. Large areas were not settled until twenty years after the negotiation of a treaty and land purchase with the Six Nations at Fort Stanwix, New York, in 1784. The agreed-upon land included the heavily timbered counties of north-central and western Pennsylvania. Sawmills were soon located throughout part of the area, but it was 1805 before one was established in Clarion County, and 1810 in Potter County.

MAKEUP OF THE FORESTS

Pennsylvania's white pine was the preferred wood of carpenters, and it was unrivaled as spar timber for making ships' masts. The commonwealth had far more hemlocks than pines, but these trees were not used for lumber until the late 1800s. Although large numbers of hemlocks were harvested for their bark, which was used in the tanning industry, often the trees themselves were left to rot. Woodworkers preferred to use pine, which was soft and easy to work with, while hemlock was harder and full of knots. This changed with the development of round, sharp, drawn nails, which went into the wood much more easily than the old square nails that they replaced. By this time, pine was becoming scarcer and more expensive, and there was great demand for wood for housing in the nation's rapidly growing cities.

Information under the title of "Report of the Forests of North America," printed as part of the tenth U.S. Census Report in 1884, stated that the vast white pine forests of Pennsylvania had almost disappeared. The report also said that some species of hardwood had been replaced by second growth, but that large growths of hemlock trees were still standing in the northern part of the state. The commonwealth still ranked second to Michigan in the value of forest products, but they were fast disappearing. By 1900, Pennsylvania still ranked fourth in lumber production, but western and southern states would soon pull ahead.

Hemlock, which made up the bulk of the remaining virgin forest and had always been the predominant tree in Pennsylvania, was finally being used by carpenters. Some had been harvested for the bark and a few other uses, but as long as more desirable trees remained, the hemlocks remained in the forests.

Potter County had some valuable stands of white pine and scattered hardwoods, but the bulk of its timber, especially in the south and west, was hemlock. Since most settlement came from the north, and the south was less suitable for agriculture, the northern tier was cleared first. Because this was headwater country with small streams, large areas were not timbered until the railroad was introduced into logging.

Harvesting of the hemlock brought about a short-lived era of prosperity in several northern counties. The tree harvest gave employment to thousands of wood hicks and barkpeelers. The patch towns that grew near the tanneries created a stable population. Both brought prosperity to the farmers, who for the first time had a nearby market for their produce.

Before the cutting started, a sea of hemlock extended across the northern part of the state, from Wayne County to Erie County. It was such an immense forest that it seemed inexhaustible, but it was removed more rapidly than the pine had been. By the turn of the cen-

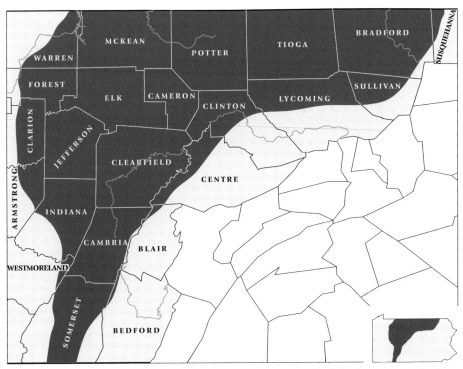

Pennsylvania's Pine and Hemlock Belt, 1881. These counties had the heaviest stands of pine and hemlock.

SHIP SPARS

Europeans coming into America, especially to Pennsylvania during the Colonial period, were not only astounded but pleased by the size of the white pine trees. In the day of wind-driven ships, these trees were valuable for masts. The spar timber found in Pennsylvania's forests made it possible to construct larger vessels, taking the world into the era of the clipper ships. Many of these carried masts cut from the commonwealth's forests.

Some pioneers who traveled into the interior looking for farmland were intimidated by the size of the white pines, but many realized that these were a source of revenue greater than what the soil could provide. As each area of pine forest was

tury, the three largest mills in Potter County alone had a combined daily capacity of more than one million board feet. Sawmills consumed the entire forest before the United States entered the Great Depression in 1929.

In addition to the pine and hemlock, many hardwood species abounded in Penn's Woods. Millions of acres were covered with oak, chestnut, maple, birch, beech, and cherry. Each species had a use in the Colonial economy. The white oak was especially important in the shipbuilding industry. Some species were quickly devoured, but others lasted for many years.

Historical Collections of Pennsylvania, published by Sherman Day in 1843, listed many of the leading forest species at the time. The north-central

settled, many of the would-be farmers became lumbermen.

Spar cutting was selective and took only the best and tallest white pines. If a spar was found to be faulty after felling, it was left to rot unless it could easily be removed to a mill for sawing. The preferred length for spars was 90 feet, but some as long as 120 feet were taken from the northern plateau. All were eighteen inches in diameter at the top end.

The men took care not to harm the spars while cutting. Several teams were used to haul each spar from the forest to a stream where it could be transported by raft to the market. Each teamster took great pride in the work that he and his horses could do, and after removing a heavy spar with a few teams, they had bragging rights until someone did a better job. Competition was keen among all the workers in the deep woods.

Most of the huge pine trees suitable for spar timber were found in the broad pine belt of northern Pennsylvania. In his "Report on the American Forests" section of the 1880 census, C. G. Pringle described this as the region drained by the headwaters of the Susquehanna, extending from Susquehanna County in the northeast through Bradford and Tioga Counties to Potter County, and then southwestward into Cameron, Elk, and Clearfield Counties. The heaviest growth in the region was on Pine Creek in the southwest part of Tioga County. Here one firm had already cut four billion feet and a little over a billion feet remained. The greatest part of the pine yet standing was on the upper waters of the West Branch of the Susquehanna in Cameron, Elk, and Clearfield counties, and this was rapidly being harvested. By the end of the nineteenth century, few stands of white pine could be found on the upper West Branch.

The valley of the upper Allegheny River, beginning in Potter County and extending westward across McKean, Warren, Clarion, and Forest Counties, produced large harvests of spar and other timber, which found its way to the western market as far away as New Orleans and northward to the New York State canals.

The largest continuous area of spar timber, and some of the last to be harvested, was located between the Clarion River on the Allegheny and Sinnemahoning Creek on the West Branch. Little of the spar timber remained in Pennsylvania's forests after 1880.

Clipper Ship. In the age of sail, spar timber from Pennsylvania's forests was used to build larger, faster ships. PENNSYLVANIA LUMBER MUSEUM

counties were denoted as primitive forests or sometimes as white pine country. Forty years later, the primeval forests of pine, hemlock, and oak were fast disappearing, and manufacturers using hardwoods complained that the material had greatly deteriorated and was becoming scarce.

Now, after three hundred years of logging, Department of Agriculture reports show that Pennsylvania's forests are productive once again. Presently, about 58 percent of Pennsylvania is forested, but only a few small tracts of the original forest remain. Today's loggers are cutting second- and third-growth trees, which are mostly hardwoods. Softwoods are a small fraction of the total. Maple, black cherry, and oaks are the leading species among the many hardwoods listed.

The Lumber Industry in Pennsylvania

Muscle power provided the energy to saw the first boards. Workmen squared the logs with a broadaxe, then placed them on a scaffold or over a hole in the ground. With one sawyer standing above the timber and the other below, they sawed the logs with a pit saw. The timber was marked with a chalk line, and because the bottom worker's position made it difficult to watch the line, it was up to the top man to keep the saw straight. A crew of two could saw one hundred board feet in a day. If greater production was needed, more men were hired. It was difficult, strenuous work, and the process was very labor-intensive, but workmen of that period were paid very low wages.

The earliest sawmills depended on water for power and became important along the interior waterways. Most of the mill, except for the saw, was made of wood. The water turned a wheel, which operated a pitman rod that caused a sash saw to move fourteen inches up and down. These mills were called up-down mills because of the working of the saw.

The first of these mills could cut about five hundred board feet per day.

As improvements were made, production doubled. After a type of gang saw that could cut several boards at one time was developed, some of these mills reached a production level of more than ten thousand board feet per day.

Both the steam engine and the circular saw were introduced into the United States from England and eventually changed the lumber industry. Because of cost, the steam mills were slow to move into the nation's interior, but as demand for lumber became greater, and because steam could operate all year round, few water mills survived very long after the Civil War.

The first steam mills used circular saws. Soon gang saws were made that cut the squared logs with one pass. Band saws with teeth on both sides further sped up the process, making it possible to cut the wood as the carriage ran in both directions. Some of the larger mills used all three types of saws and developed previously unheard-of capacities. A few hemlock mills exceeded two hundred thousand board feet per day. Even though most sawmills did not work to capacity, the forests that had survived into the 1880s disappeared rapidly.

Pennsylvania's Bountiful Forests fueled the state's lumber industry—and created strenuous work for lumberjacks, who cut trees by hand with saws and axes. PENNSYLVANIA LUMBER MUSEUM

The Circular Saw, a British innovation, helped revolutionize the lumber industry. PENNSYLVANIA LUMBER MUSEUM

The Band Saw, another advance in log cutting. Some had teeth on both sides, boosting capacity. POTTER COUNTY HISTORICAL SOCIETY

Up-Down Sawmill. *Its water-powered vertical movement gave this type of sawmill its name.*
PENNSYLVANIA LUMBER MUSEUM

The Gang Saw, *like this one from McKean County, enabled mills to multiply their production.* POTTER COUNTY HISTORICAL SOCIETY

RAFTING

The early lumber industry transported its products by rafting them on waterways. In addition to log and square-timber rafts, boards, shingles, staves and headings, and other wood products reached the markets by water. During the earliest period, spars were the most valuable products rafted. Rafting began on the North Branch of the Susquehanna in 1807 and on the West Branch a few years later. In the northern and western parts of the state, products were rafted on the Allegheny River.

After about thirty years, rafting reached its peak, and lumber towns grew along the rivers. By the 1830s, two thousand to twenty-five hundred log and hewn timber rafts started from the Susquehanna headwaters with each spring flood, destined to reach the tidewater and the chief distribution point at Port Deposit, Maryland. Most of this rafted timber was used in the Philadelphia area, but some rafts were towed to New York City. On the Allegheny, most of the rafts traveled to Pittsburgh, but some floated all the way to New

Rafting. Water was essential to the lumber industry, not just for power but also for transportation. In the early years and for some time afterward, rafting was a common method of moving logs and finished products. PENNSYLVANIA LUMBER MUSEUM

Orleans. Sometimes, the greatest adventure was the long journey home, from the mouth of the Mississippi in Louisiana to the source of the Allegheny in Potter County, Pennsylvania. The Delaware River was also the highway for several hundred million board feet of lumber rafts each year.

Raftsmen were considered the elite of the lumber industry. Every young woodsman sought an opportunity to take the dangerous ride, especially those living on the headwater streams, who could ride the spring freshets several hundred miles to the tidewater. Stories of the dangers seemed not to frighten but to challenge these young men, who knew that many of the swift-moving headwater rafts had stoved against the sharp curves on rocky banks, causing the loss of both life and property. On the rapid waters, the rafts sometimes seemed to move faster than the stream itself, making them very difficult to control. Rafts were piloted by seasoned experts who, eventually, turned

the dangerous trips over to those young men waiting in the wings. The making of rafts was time-consuming and expensive, but if the trips were successful, they brought a good profit.

Initially, the lumber sold at a fairly low price. Select pine cost $7.50 per thousand board feet, hemlock brought as little as $1.00, and some other species were priced at a few dollars. Pine shingles sold for $1.50 per thousand board feet. Prices increased after both producers and customers began to realize that the forests were not inexhaustible. By 1878, both logs and manufactured lumber cost $8 per thousand board feet.

THE WEST BRANCH AND LOG BOOMS

For well over a century, the West Branch of the Susquehanna and its largest tributary, Sinnemahoning Creek, resounded with the echo of the woodsman's axe. From 1820 until 1900, its two-hundred-mile length from Cambria County to Northumberland County, where it joins the North Branch, was Pennsylvania's last primeval forest, and the source of much of the nation's lumber supply. It was the wildest, most mountainous portion of the state, an area so rugged that most of it was avoided by the farmers, leaving sections to be settled by the lumbermen. Other river areas had been prolific in forest products, but for years the principal scene was here.

White pine spar timbers were the first to be sent from the headwaters of the West Branch, but later hemlock and various hardwoods were rafted and splashed to downriver mills. Lock Haven, at the northern end of the Bald Eagle Canal, was the first town of size to depend upon the forest business. Many thought that the canal should be extended up the Sinnemahoning and on to Erie, but the rugged terrain halted construction north of Farrandsville. Before work was continued from there, a new source of transportation—the railroad—was available to the logger.

As the timber harvest increased, some people were concerned that the growing raft traffic was becoming more dangerous. One of these men, James H. Perkins from New Hampshire, developed and constructed a great log boom at Williamsport, Pennsylvania. The log boom was a form of corral made by connecting log and stone cribs with chained-together logs. One side of the river was left open for raft traffic. Each of the loose logs was identified by a mark of the owner placed on each end with a hammer. The marks were registered at the Lycoming County Courthouse, and each log with its particular mark was credited to the owner when sorted by the boom workers.

The boom brought such prosperity to Williamsport that it became the leading sawmill city in the nation, and for a time, it was known as the lumber capital of the world. In 1860, Pennsylvania led the nation in lumber production. For the next two decades, it was second only to Michigan, and even in 1900, when the original forests had been nearly depleted, Pennsylvania was still fourth in the nation.

The Susquehanna (Log) Boom Company, as Perkins's boom was known, was incorporated March 26, 1846, and a facility was erected to collect the logs that would be floated downstream. It was three years before the boom was in operation. At the boom, the logs were sorted by workers called boom rats and distributed to the more than thirty sawmills that had located there. Over the next two decades, booms were put in place at Loyalsock, Linden, Lock Haven, Jersey Shore, Montoursville, and Muncy. These booms handled billions of logs before they closed just before World War I. Today most evidence of their existence is gone, except for a few of the cribs that were connected by boom chains at Williamsport.

The greatest threat to the Williamsport boom was flooding. In 1860, it was broken and almost fifty million board feet of lumber was carried downstream. That summer, fifty-four new cribs were added, but damage the next spring was also heavy. In 1861, the boom at Lock Haven broke, and the logs were carried downstream with great force, damaging the Linden and Williamsport facilities. The greatest flood occurred on June 1, 1889, when three hundred million feet of logs were carried away.

When the log booms were first put into operation, the practice of floating logs encountered violent opposition. At a meeting held in a Snow Shoe schoolhouse, an address set forth the grievances and detailed the injurious results of loose logs in the streams. The hearing determined that these logs were "hazards to our person and property and the practice of floating logs in Moshannon

Log Boom. *Logs sent downstream were collected at log booms and distributed to nearby mills. This boom belonged to the Dodge Mill and stood near Williamsport.*
PENNSYLVANIA LUMBER MUSEUM

THE SAWDUST WAR

During more than fifty years of operation, only one serious episode of labor unrest occurred at Williamsport. The season of 1872 was one of high timber production, sending an enormous stock of logs to the mills, which had to run overtime to keep ahead of the supply. Some mill crews had to work twelve- or fourteen-hour days, leaving little time for rest. As a result, employees formed an organization and asked for a ten-hour workday. This was refused, so a strike was called on June 29.

Several mills resumed operations with men who had deserted the strike force along with some new men. This incited the strike leaders to attack the working mills and drive away the employees. Several men were injured, and strikers threatened to burn the lumberyards. The mill owners appealed to Pennsylvania governor John W. Geary for military aid, which he granted. Some of the strikers were arrested, and order was quickly restored. Twenty-one men were tried, of whom seventeen were given light sentences. When the other four were taken to prison, they were pardoned by the governor and released.

This strike, which lasted for three weeks, has been referred to as the "Sawdust War." It appears to have been the only serious difficulty between the commonwealth's lumber companies and their employees.

Creek shall from this night cease." A committee was appointed to stop the practice, peacefully if possible, forcibly if necessary. A few years later, in June 1857, the *Potter Journal*, a local newspaper, noted an act passed by the Pennsylvania Legislature: From that time, "if any person shall place any stumps, loose saw logs, or fallen trees, in the West Branch of the Susquehanna River above the mouth of the Sinnemahoning Creek and including said creek or convey any logs, lumber, spars of timber of any kind, unless the same be sufficiently rafted or loaded in Arks or Boats, the person so offending shall pay for every such offense the sum of ten dollars to the county treasurer where the offense occurred." The second section of the act stated that "any person desirous of floating of saw logs on the streams" must apply to the court for a license to do so. The license could be renewed annually.

Rafts continued their journeys in lesser numbers as more loose logs were floated during this especially busy era on the rivers. Preparation for a log drive took much less time than building a raft, and many more logs could be taken downriver during a season. Also, the headwater streams, by using splash dams, could get the logs down to the river. Driving required a large crew and many horses to keep the logs in the streams as they passed the splash, but the practice proved successful and accounted for billions of logs floating downstream over the next fifty years, before the railroads took over the transportation of forest products.

Sometimes difficulties arose between the drivers and raftsmen. Perhaps the most destructive practice was that of driving spikes into the floating logs, which raftsmen did to retaliate against log drivers. This was called "ironing." If a mill put a spiked log through a saw, the saw and other equipment could be ruined and workers injured, so the mills would refuse to saw the whole shipment of floating logs. The spiking led to the peeling of all logs that were to be floated so that any iron would be visible. The peeling was more advantageous to the drivers; jams were one of the greatest dangers they faced, and peeled logs did not jam

Log Driving *required a large number of teams to keep logs moving but was less time-consuming and more productive than rafting.* PENNSYLVANIA LUMBER MUSEUM

Commissary Ark. *While logs were floated down waterways, workers ate in floating messes like this on Little Pine Creek.* PENNSYLVANIA LUMBER MUSEUM

as easily. Although Perkins had thought that the log drives would be less hazardous than rafting, both were dangerous, and few seasons passed when lives were not lost on wrecked rafts or at jams that had to be broken up by the drivers.

RAILROADS

Railroads carried products from the lumbermills to the market for a few years before the log train was introduced to the harvesting of timber. As improvements were made to logging equipment during the Civil War period, a few lumbermen began to experiment with horse-drawn cars and some with simple engines. History credits the first logging railroad to Jefferson County, Pennsylvania, in 1864, but it was about twenty years before the rails began to really be noticed in the forests, and a few more years before this method of transport reached its peak of proficiency. Much of Pennsylvania's forests along the streams

had been harvested, but some areas of the deep forests remained. With the advent of the steam railroad, it became possible to penetrate into these isolated areas and also to manufacture logs into lumber in the backwoods. Mills near the timberland grew to become some of the largest in the nation.

Some areas of hardwood remained to be carried to the mills by rail. Other timber not used for lumber was purchased by chemical plants and taken to their facilities by rail. When hemlock was cut, logs were carried by day and the bark was transported to the tanneries at night.

The railroads were particularly successful on tributary streams that were too small for splashing logs. The main line would be built up the larger stream, which had been timbered earlier, and side lines were laid up to the head of the first small stream. As each tributary was harvested, the tracks were taken up and

The Railroad helped the lumber industry reach previously isolated forests, but main-line locomotives could not traverse the steep, rugged terrain. Special engines, such as these Shays, were designed for that purpose. PENNSYLVANIA LUMBER MUSEUM

The Steam-Powered Log Loader accelerated the slow, dangerous work of loading logs and enabled logs to be placed easily on railroad cars. PENNSYLVANIA LUMBER MUSEUM

moved to the next one. This procedure was used until the entire watershed was stripped. Loggers thus made rapid work of the harvest of the last of Pennsylvania's virgin forest. Within a few decades, the north-central mountains were a vast, cut-over wasteland.

Although the railroad allowed the rapid transport of logs, loading remained slow. Throughout much of the logging era, the wood hicks had moved and loaded logs using a peavey. This was hard, difficult, dangerous work, and preparing a decked log landing for loading was slow. If men hurried, more accidents occurred, killing some and maiming many others. Logging was one of the most dangerous occupations, and it remains so today.

The invention that improved the lot of the hick was the idea of Frank H. Goodyear, who came from Buffalo, New York, to the Allegheny-Susquehanna headwaters to harvest the hemlock forests. He was among the first to use

railroads on this part of the plateau, and it was his idea that brought the Barnhart steam logloader into use. He was cutting and sawing more than a hundred million board feet of hemlock per year in an area of difficult topography, and he wanted a machine to speed up the work.

Goodyear approached the Marion Steam Power Shovel Company, of Marion, Ohio, which developed a loader that could pick up logs from a rough-and-tumble landing using a small crew. The loader was mounted on rails on top of the log car and could move along as it loaded the logs. Equipped with a cable boom, it picked up logs on either side of the track. The invention proved successful, and the Goodyears purchased more than forty loaders. It was not long before other companies were using the loader, and competitions became common among crews to see who could load the most logs in the shortest time.

Engines used on the main lines could not travel on the steep grades used by the loggers, so special-geared engines were developed for this purpose. Three types were used in Pennsylvania. Of these, perhaps the most popular was the Shay, manufactured by Lima Machine Works in Lima, Ohio. Two others, the Climax and the Heisler, were manufactured in northwestern Pennsylvania. By the end of World War I, with lumbering in Pennsylvania slowing down and moving south and west, most of the geared engines had been sold to western and southern logging railroads. Probably the last to be used in the commonwealth was at Sheffield, where the operation was closed in 1945, but the hauling had been taken over by motor trucks about ten years earlier.

LARGER-CAPACITY SAWMILLS

After the Civil War, more circular saws and steam-operated mills with much greater capacities were brought into the headwaters. Although rafts were floated on Pine, Kettle, and Sinnemahoning Creeks and the Allegheny River for years, the smaller streams were not used until after the log booms were built on the Susquehanna River and loose logs were floated to Williamsport and nearby booms. Since almost two-thirds of Potter County is in the Susquehanna watershed, harvesting of timber in these areas increased. Splash dams were built where there was plentiful water to create a splash. Potter County timber helped make Williamsport a lumber city, but tracts of hemlock along the smaller streams were intact.

There were a few larger-capacity mills in Hebron, Sharon, and nearby townships, and a number were located on Pine Creek. Some with a daily capacity of twenty thousand board feet were appearing, but transportation of the finished product to the market remained

a problem. Absentee landlords would solve this situation, and within a few decades, southern Potter County was cut over.

What was formerly inaccessible land was made accessible with the introduction of the railroad. The change took place after the Goodyear Lumber Company, with headquarters in Buffalo, New York, purchased large tracts of hemlock and hardwoods along Pine, Kettle, and Sinnemahoning Creeks. The timber areas lay far enough away from the main streams that they had been overlooked by previous developers. After the purchase was completed, the company constructed the large sawmills at the very threshold of the forests and arranged for electric lighting to make it possible to operate twenty-four hours a day. Starting at midnight on Sunday, the mills would run continuously until midnight on Saturday. Each day was divided into two eleven-hour shifts, with an hour between to make adjustments.

A great profit factor for the company was the sale of hemlock bark to the tanneries. When the Austin mill was constructed, the large Costello tannery had already been operating. Goodyear's logging trains would carry logs to the mills during the daytime hours and bark to the tannery at night. They cut the hemlock and sold the hardwoods on their land to companies that specialized in cutting maple, oak, and cherry. At both Austin and Galeton, the Emporium Lumber Company had a mill to process the hardwoods.

To show the magnitude of the lumber industry in the commonwealth and the milling methods used during the latter part of the nineteenth century, the U.S. Department of Agriculture included the following information in an annual report published in 1897.

The operations described were those of F. H. and C. W. Goodyear of Buffalo, New York, at Austin and Galeton, and those of the Lackawanna Lumber Company from Scranton, Pennsylvania, located at Cross Fork. At the time, the Goodyear mill at Austin was the largest in the state, and the Lackawanna mill was one of the larger operations. Both companies were noted for the use of modern methods and innovative machinery.

The companies operated near each other, but the Lackawanna holdings were farther south. The Goodyear mill was somewhat larger, but the methods used to harvest and mill the timber were about the same as at similar large operations throughout the state. Goodyear was more into railroading and added a line to its Buffalo and Susquehanna Railroad to transport the Lacakawanna Company's lumber out of Cross Fork. They also helped operate logging roads.

Large crews of men and many teams of horses were used in the cutting operations, but both companies employed large machines for loading and carrying logs for the mill. At the time of the report, Goodyear had twenty-four hundred men working in the woods. Fifteen hundred of these were needed during bark-peeling season. The company owned five Shay engines (more were purchased later), 207 log cars, and eleven log loaders. All of the harvest work was left to fifteen jobbers, who sublet part of their contracts to others. Altogether, the contractors had forty camps in the woods to house workmen.

The trees were first cut down, peeled, then cut into log lengths and skidded to skidways near the railroads using horses. If this area was too steep or rugged for the horses, slides consisting of three logs placed side by side and hewn out in the center were made as long as required for the area. The logs were taken to the skidways much more rapidly in this manner. In summer, the slides were lubricated with heavy oil, causing the logs to move very rapidly. During the winter, the slides were iced. Descending logs would

Felling Trees long remained a labor-intensive process, even as technology quickened the moving of logs and the cutting of boards, PENNSYLVANIA LUMBER MUSEUM

SHEFFIELD

The northern and central plateau of Pennsylvania was covered with hemlock forests. These were a great source of tannin, which was used by tanneries for the leathermaking process, so tanneries located near areas where the trees were being cut. After a time, many of the private tanneries were purchased by the United States Leather Company, and a virtual monopoly was formed that depended on the lumbermen for their supply of tannin. As the forests were harvested, the company became concerned about its future supply, so it began to purchase as many of the hemlock tracts as possible. As the twentieth century approached, much of the remaining virgin timber was owned by the leather company, which had up until this time depended upon private companies for the harvesting of the timber and bark.

Realizing they owned much of the remaining hemlock, the owners of the leather trust, being businessmen, decided that they should cut and saw their own timber and increase their profit. To do this, they organized the Central Pennsylvania Lumber Company (CPL), which was incorporated at Williamsport on April 29, 1903. Soon they not only were in the tanning and hemlock lumber businesses, but they also were cutting hardwoods. (It is important to note, however, that while tanneries and sawmills were parallel industries in this case, not all sawmills were connected with a tannery.)

Their mills were operated at Loleta, Leetonia, Galeton, Costello, Jamison City, and other locations, but their largest and longest-lasting operation was at Sheffield in eastern Warren County. The village was served by the Tionesta Valley and Pennsylvania Railroads and was near one of the company's largest tracts. It was the perfect location for the company to build a mill. The valley here was wider than those farther east, making room for a sawmill of tremendous capacity.

The town of Sheffield was already an established area with several forest-related industries when CPL began its operation, which would assure growth and stability for a few more decades. With a capacity of more than 130,000 board feet of lumber in eight hours, the mill was planned to be one of the largest in the state, but it seldom worked more than one shift per day. In most of the other mills, the crews worked two eleven-hour shifts, thus increasing their daily output. The Warren newspaper reported that on March 14, 1923, the Sheffield mill sawed 337,074 board feet of hemlock logs in ten hours. The nearby forests would have been devoured even more rapidly if the mill had used two shifts.

The sawmill began operation about three years after the company was organized and sawed until July 1941. CPL's nearby hardwood mill had closed in 1930, just one year before the company's offices were moved from Williamsport to Sheffield.

Until 1935, CPL used the railroads to transport logs from the forest to its mill, making it the last company to extensively use the train to harvest timber. For the last six years, trucks were used, marking the beginning of a new era in the history of lumbering.

Central Pennsylvania Lumber Company's Sheffield Mill was the largest and most modern double band mill to operate in the state. PENNSYLVANIA LUMBER MUSEUM

Sawing. After trees were felled and before they were skidded to loading areas, wood-hicks cut them into pieces ten to twenty feet in length to ease handling. PENNSYLVANIA LUMBER MUSEUM

sometimes reach the velocity of a cannonball and shoot through the air for hundreds of feet. Both the skidding of logs and the stocking of slides were dangerous for the men and horses. If jobbers thought that the speed of the logs created too much danger, the slide would be spiked to check the velocity of the logs. Using the old method of loading, the logs had to be piled in rows on the skidway, but for the log loader, they could be piled in any manner and did not have to be as close to the tracks. The cars operated on the company's seventy-five miles of logging railroads.

Goodyear had two mills at Austin, called the large and small. The largest was a two-story frame structure 60 feet wide and 230 feet long. The inside was whitewashed to help the lighting, which was provided by a large dynamo. The mill was equipped with two band saws, one fifty-inch Wicks Brothers' gang saw, two edgers containing eight saws each, two slashers with five saws, and one trimmer containing fourteen saws. The logs were brought from the pond, where they had been unloaded from the cars,

Log Slide. Logs were easily transported from the forest through the use of makeshift slides. Here workers build a slide in Potter County. PENNSYLVANIA LUMBER MUSEUM

to the jack ladder by means of an end-less chain containing sharp prongs. From the log deck, they were then thrown down to the center deck by a special machine, and from there loaded into the saw carriage. For turning the log on the carriage, a steam log turner was used. Much of the equipment was made by Clark Brothers of Belmont, New York.

The band saws were run by twin engines fed by special equipment. The other machinery was run by belt pulleys or rope. In most mills, movement was entirely by the use of belts, but in this mill, it was by means of ropes. The saw carriage was moved back and forth by steam or friction feed, which was under the control of the sawyer. To run the carriage, two men were needed, a sawyer and a setter.

The circular saw was operated in the same manner, but in this mill, more lumber was cut with the band saw. It made less sawdust and straighter lumber, and it was believed it could cut more lumber. The slabs from the boards were carried to the slasher, cut into four-foot lengths, and sent to a kindling wood factory, which in this case was nearby.

The small mill at Austin had a capacity of two hundred thousand board feet in twenty-two hours, but at the time of the census report, it had been operating only during the daytime. This mill was equipped with one band saw, a circular saw, an edger with eight saws, one slasher with five saws, and a trimmer containing fourteen saws. The fuel used was sawdust, and the small bits of lumber were used by the kindling wood factory. Any other refuse was burned in a brick burner. To keep the ponds that were used for the logs from freezing during the winter, the exhaust steam from the engines fed into the pond. The operations were basically the same in both mills.

The Goodyear mill at Galeton was operated by H. W. Sullivan, who also had been in charge at Austin. This mill had a daily capacity of 220,000 board feet in twenty-two hours, with an annual capacity of sixty million feet. The timber cut was hemlock, harvested from the headwaters of Pine Creek.

The engine was rated at 470 horse-power and had four additional boilers of 150 horsepower each. The room contained a large dynamo, which was capable of furnishing twelve hundred electric lights for the mill at night. This was twice the number needed.

In all three Goodyear mills, a "hog" machine was used to grind refuse into sawdust to make sure the fires were kept going. The other refuse at Galeton was burned in a twenty-foot-diameter water-jacketed burner that was seventy feet high. The mills each had a room equipped for saw sharpening and repair. There was also a repair room for belting and general mill maintenance. The mill employed 140 men, not including those who worked on the docks and the logging railroad.

Since 1893, two mills had been maintained by the Lackawanna Lumber Company at Cross Fork. The company had purchased forty thousand acres of hemlock and mixed hardwood timber and expected to operate for fifteen years. The company built some of its own logging roads and had limited equipment, which included two Shay locomotives, one rod locomotive, and seventy log cars. The finished lumber was taken to market on the Buffalo and Susquehanna or Goodyear line, built in 1893.

The two mills, called twin mills, stood side by side. They were among the most commodious in the state, with a combined capacity of five million board feet per month or sixty million per year. During the winter, the smaller mill sawed only hardwood, working two shifts. The big mill sawed only hemlock. The only other large industry in the village was a stave mill operated by the Pennsylvania Stave Company.

The mills used a variety of equipment of a modern type similar to Goodyear's. They had one large circular saw, two band saws, one gang saw containing thirty-eight saws, three edgers containing eight saws each, two slashers with six saws, and two eight-saw trimmers. In addition, they operated lath machines. The circular saw and the band saws operated by steam feed and the other machines by belt.

The gang machinery was made by Wm. Wicks of Saginaw, Michigan, and was said to have manufactured perfect lumber. It was capable of sawing one hundred thousand feet of one-inch lumber in ten hours. The lumber was carried from one machine to another by a system of live rolls and transfer chains. The refuse was carried to the lath mill, where a majority was made into four-foot lath.

Lackawanna mills employed eighty men, but all of their operations had a payroll containing 350 workers. The Cross Fork work was under the direction of C. P. Davidson. This mill complex, except for the docks and lumber, was destroyed by fire early on January 1, 1900, but within a few months, it was reconstructed with a greater capacity. It ran until April 30, 1903, when a fire destroyed the mills and fourteen million board feet of lumber. A new double-band sawmill was in place and sawing by the end of September. In the next five years, this mill completed the cutting of the original tract plus several thousand more acres. During 1908, the last logs were cut, and the Lackawanna operation left Pennsylvania and moved south.

The stave mill worked a few more years before closing. The railroad was taken up in 1912, and nature began to reclaim the Kettle Creek Valley.

Logging Camps grew up near the forests in order to house workers. PENNSYLVANIA LUMBER MUSEUM

GHOST TOWNS

The size of a sawmill town depended on the size of the mill, which depended on the size of the tract. Most areas of the hemlock forests had mill towns with a few rows of houses and a couple hundred inhabitants, but a few towns became well established and had several thousand people. After the lumber era ended, some lumbering towns and cities, such as Williamsport, Lock Haven, and Dubois, were able to adapt to new and different industries. Some of these towns not only survived, but grew. The homes of successful lumber barons, such as those in Williamsport, remind present residents of their heritage, but little else of the early lumber era remains. Other lumbering towns were abandoned and are now ghost towns.

The Lackawanna Lumber Company, based at Scranton, had a small village at the mill at Mina on the Allegheny River and a substantial town at the large mill on Kettle Creek at Cross Fork. A few structures survive at each location but little is left to indicate this early activity. Cross Fork, located on the Potter–Clinton County border, was the home of nearly two thousand people in 1900, but ten years later, all was gone. The location is now the site of a tiny village with small outlet stores and restaurants. The total population of the township of Stewardson, in which the town is located, is about one hundred permanent residents.

Loleta, in western Elk County, was once the scene of an operation of the Central Pennsylvania Lumber Company. It was smaller than Cross Fork and few people lived there who did not work at the mill. Its one store, which was next to the mill, was the center of activity. There townsfolk could purchase all necessities, food, clothing, and hardware, and when picking up their mail, they could get caught up on the local gossip.

Travelers came and went via the Tionesta Valley Railroad, which carried freight, logs, and passengers to Sheffield. Any person who wished to communicate with the outside world had to use the only phone in town, which was located in the sawmill office. Loleta was not a wild town, like a few of the mill towns. There was little activity in the village, which had three boardinghouses but no movies, dances, radios, or saloons. As there was no night life, there was no need for a policeman. On Sundays, a minister preached a sermon in a room above the company store.

As the timber was harvested and the mill slowed operations, the company began to transfer the men to its other mills. In a short time, all activity at Loleta ceased, and nature began to reclaim the land.

In southeastern Bradford County, Laquin not only was a sawmill town, but it also contained many other related wood industries. Very little was wasted. The hemlocks supplied the sawmill, and a variety of hardwoods also made it possible for the town to have a chemical plant, a stave mill, a hub factory, and a veneer plant. In addition, the bark was shipped to area tanneries.

For the first ten years, Barclay Brothers operated the mill for the tanning industry. Then it closed for a short time until it was purchased by the Central Pennsylvania Lumber Company. This company's land in several nearby counties kept operations going for another ten years or more.

In spite of its isolated location, Laquin had about 110 large stuccoed homes that were supplied with electricity and running water, as well as several stores, two schools, churches, lodges, boardinghouses, and a hotel. All of this activity filled the narrow valley for almost thirty years. This now unpopulated area was once the second-largest manufacturing community in Bradford County. The only buildings there today are hunting camps, and many of those who fish Schrader Creek or hunt in one of the state game lands in the valley do not realize how busy the area was just one hundred years ago.

The best stories of the deserted villages and ghost towns of Pennsylvania are found in a series of books called *Logging Railroad Era of Lumbering in Pennsylvania* (see the Further Reading section).

LOGGING CAMPS

After the railroads began to haul the timber to the mills and the lumber to the market, it was no longer necessary to have the mills located near the booms, and sawmills were built near the large timber tracts. A mill would cut until all the timber had been harvested, and then it would be closed down permanently or moved to locate near another timber stand. This meant the movement of many people. First to go were those who harvested the timber, then those who operated the mill, and finally those who provided services, if the town was large enough to require amenities.

Besides the sawmill towns, which grew up next to the mills, logging camps were built near the timber. These camps were temporary communities, sometimes located deep in the forest. The hicks who cut the trees, peeled the bark, and skidded the logs to the railroad lived there. The earlier camps of the spar timber era lasted for several years and had more of an appearance of permanence than the later hemlock camps, which usually lasted just one season before being moved. The smaller pine camps had one-story log buildings, whereas the hemlock camps had larger, two-story buildings made of rough boards. Camp size was determined by the number of hicks needed by the jobber, who was contracted by the timber owner to harvest a particular tract within a certain timeframe, to complete a job.

Clyde Lynch, a Port Allegany teacher, describes the camp buildings used by his father during the early twentieth century as sixteen feet wide with one foot of length for each man who was to live there. The camp's main building had a capacity of one hundred men and was one hundred feet long. It had a kitchen, store, lobby, office, and dining area down-

Mess Hall. *Camps met the basic but important needs of a lumber crew. In the mess hall, the men ate hearty meals, often in silence.*
PENNSYLVANIA LUMBER MUSEUM

stairs and sleeping quarters upstairs. This camp had double beds in which two men slept, but in some areas the hicks refused to sleep with one another and used single beds. If they had to use double beds, they cut a pole to fit down the center between the sleepers. With only one window in each end of the sleeping area under the roof, it was very hot during the summer.

Each jobber owned about ten teams or hired teamsters who owned their horses, so a barn was an important part of the camp. The horses were shod in a separate shop by the blacksmith, who made and repaired iron tools, chains, harnesses, and anything else that was brought his way. The cutting was done with a cross-cut saw, and to keep the saw sharp, each camp had a filer, who often had his own little building. Some camps had a separate building where the jobber and his family lived. A woods boss, hired by the jobber to oversee the tree cutting, most often lived with the crew.

To keep a good crew, a camp needed an excellent cook. The life of the wood hick mostly consisted of working, eating, and sleeping, and a bad cook could drive them away to seek a camp where the food was better. Each cook had one or more helpers called "cookees." As the industry moved into the twentieth century, more women were employed as cooks, often the wife of the jobber.

Another person who helped in the camp was the lobbyhog, who kept the lobby and sleeping quarters picked up. In some camps, he did a lot of cleaning. As bedbugs and lice could easily invade a camp, the lobbyhog sometimes sprayed the beds with kerosene. In some camps, little effort was made to control the bugs, and the crews accepted them, saying, "They can bite and be damned." Cleaner camps kept a wash boiler of hot water, where the clothing could be deloused.

Bundlers. Although few women worked in lumber camps, some worked in kindling wood factories as bundlers. PENNSYLVANIA LUMBER MUSEUM

Swampers were employed to make and repair roads used to take the peeled bark to the railroad. All hemlock had to be peeled before the Fourth of July, when the bark would become tight on the tree. This marked the end of the season for the peelers.

Few people from the outside ventured to the camp, so entertainment was of the men's own making. It was quite simple: a little music, some storytelling, playing cards, and a lot of smoking and tobacco spitting. Occasionally during the season, a peddler would visit the camp, or perhaps an itinerant preacher or photographer would come to the camp. For long periods, no one came except the merchants and farmers who sold supplies and produce. Supplying the camps became a profitable business and flourished as long as they existed. The lobby store sold socks and a few necessities, but tobacco products were their best sellers.

On Sundays at the camp, the men rested, washed clothes, and sharpened their axes. Those with families away from the area often wrote letters. The teamsters spent time caring for their horses.

Many teamsters went to the barn to tend to their horses whenever they had a few minutes to themselves. To some, the horses were better company than the men. Henry Eckert, who spent thirty years as a teamster, says that they arose before the rest of the crew. "When we heard the cook downstairs, we got up. We did not wake the rest of the men. We had to feed our horses and get them ready in the morning. Also, after you came in at night and ate dinner, you had to go out and work on them. At the end of the day, I watered the horses and gave them oats. After supper, I went out and washed them. Teamsters were paid $1.50 or $1.60 per day."

Some members of the crew never left camp during the season. They did not collect any pay until the job was completed, and then they headed for home and their families. For woodsmen who liked competition, the end of the season was a time to get together and show off their skills. Some went to the nearest town and spent their money on liquor and fights before returning broke to camp. They had to be rugged individuals, for if they were hurt in a fight or on the job, there was no first aid. Only if a bone was broken or a person was near death was a doctor called.

LUMBER DYNASTIES

The era of the water-powered sawmill involved many facilities, harvesting small tracts that combined to take millions of board feet from the region. Few dynasties were formed before the steam era, although some operations harvested the spar timber, pine, and oak, removing previously unheard-of volumes of trees.

Pre–Civil War lumbering was a vast, intense operation, and much of eastern and southeastern Pennsylvania was stripped of the primeval forest. As operations moved into the interior, the commonwealth became a competitor on the lumber market. Its operations ranked third in the nation in 1840, second in 1850, and first in 1860. The vast plateau country was then yielding its timber to the market.

One of the first northern Pennsylvania lumber dynasties began here in 1835, when William E. Dodge purchased land in Tioga County. Within a few years, this company was putting three million board feet of lumber through its mills annually. Dodge formed a partnership with Anson Phelps, which became Phelps, Dodge and Company, employing five hundred

men in the woods and mills. Using water-powered gang saws, they sawed thousands of board feet each day. In addition, each spring they sent out one hundred board rafts downriver to tidewater. After the opening of the booms on the Susquehanna, they opened a mill on Pine Creek just above Jersey Shore, putting them closer to the downriver markets. After fifteen years, Phelps, Dodge agents began to appear on the Sinnemahoning.

Both Phelps and Dodge were religious men and were concerned about the spiritual well-being of their employees. Therefore, they hired men to manage their enterprises whom they thought would follow Christian principles.

In 1850, they hired Hiram Pritchard to manage their store at Sinnemahoning. Almost immediately, he began to complain about a lack of cooperation and wrote, "I believe there are few men here who will speak the truth and sin not." He put a stop to the sale of whiskey at the store and suspended business on Sunday. He felt that with a few changes, Sinnemahoning could be made into a respectable, God-fearing community. Pritchard progressed against intemperance and inefficiency and was made chief agent for the company on the Sinnemahoning.

Insights into Dodge's character may be gleaned from his first trip to the Pine Creek area, when he stopped at Williamsport and inquired about a church and Sunday school. He not only attended and spoke to the congregation during an afternoon meeting, but was asked to speak at an evening service. He continued his dedication to the honorable life throughout his career.

After the death of Anson Phelps in 1853, Dodge remained with the company for another ten years before turn-

BARK PEELERS' CONVENTION

The Bark Peelers' Convention is one of the annual events at the Pennsylvania Lumber Museum. The convention is a reenactment of the Fourth of July gatherings held by wood-hicks a century ago and features regional food and music, as well as various lumber industry demonstrations. Greased pole, tobacco spitting, birling, fiddling, and frog jumping contests are held. Contact the site for more information on the event and other programs held throughout the year (see page 47).

ART BECKER

ART BECKER

ART BECKER

ing his Pennsylvania interests over to his son. He continued to operate lumber interests in Canada and Georgia for a few years.

Two years after Dodge first visited Williamsport, another lumberman came to town. John Dubois, Jr., had been in the lumber business near the headwaters of the North Branch of the Susquehanna in New York State. As a young man, he showed business ability after being

placed in charge of his father's raft fleet. He not only was successful at selling the rafts above the market price, but also proved to be imaginative in developing techniques to be used in cutting and sawing lumber.

In 1838, he and his brothers purchased timberland and a mill along Lycoming Creek above Williamsport. They operated there for about fifteen years, until the brothers died, leaving

John on his own. He purchased and developed two farms on the south side of the river opposite Williamsport, where he built a large steam gang saw mill. The venture was profitable, and the town that grew around the mill became Duboistown. Dubois was interested in the Boom Company and served as one of its officers.

After difficulties with competition and labor at Williamsport led to some bad feelings, Dubois disposed of his property and moved to northern Clearfield County, where he had purchased timberland years before.

The move led to increased success, and he became one of the largest operators in the state, both in harvesting and milling. As new methods were developed, he was often one of the first to use them. His use of the logging railroad led to increased production, and in 1874, he constructed the largest sawmill in the commonwealth. This mill had a capacity of five hundred thousand board feet per day and was built at the second town to use his name. This second town, Dubois, became much larger than the first.

When Dubois's operations began there, the site had three houses. Three sawmills, a box factory, and other company operations brought in other related industries, and soon Dubois became a busy town. Within a decade, it was a city of seven thousand people. When John Dubois died in 1886, his property and assets were valued at more than $8 million.

Throughout Pennsylvania, those who invested in timber met with different degrees of success. All of the successful ones were shrewd, ambitious businessmen of various degrees of wealth. Those who left a real legacy were men of outstanding character, in some cases almost folk heroes, such as Truman D. Collins.

Like many who came to northern Pennsylvania, Teddy Collins, who kept his childhood nickname for life, was born in New York State and moved southward as a young man. During his first thirty-three years, he had achieved success in several enterprises before coming to Forest County in 1854 to become a lumberman. Not only was he successful again, but he became one of the area's most respected citizens.

Of all the great lumbermen in Pennsylvania, Collins is one of the best remembered, admired, and respected. He was almost a mythical character in the annals of Forest County. All of his life, he was a devout Christian first and a businessman second. He considered all his possessions as given him in trust by God. It was his duty to manage them as a steward and for the kingdom of God. He was a Methodist whose hobby, one might say, was building churches for the benefit of his employees.

Collins bought timber tracts in Forest County, chiefly along the Tionesta Creek. He had mills at Tynedale, Nebraska, Golinza, Bucks Mills, and Kelletville, among others. Because the stream joined the Allegheny River at Tionesta Borough, the lumber was moved by water, but as time passed, logging railroads were established throughout the watershed. The entire area was a beehive of activity from the Civil War until after the turn of the century.

Additionally, Collins invested in another important lumber industry in the Clarion River–Tionesta area: the building of barges and boats that were used in the Pittsburgh trade and on the Ohio River. Here again, white pine was the lumber of choice, and business continued until the timber was used up after World War I.

Few men ever achieved what Teddy Collins did after reaching sixty years of age. He had several partners, but he never gave up his interest in the business. He was a familiar sight at both his mills and wood jobs. During the next twenty years, he tripled his timber holdings and added four sawmills. His mills were eventually cutting more than fifty million board feet per year.

Nathan P. Wheeler was a contemporary of Collins's for the last thirty years of the nineteenth century. He came to Forest County in 1871 and developed a similar reputation. He was a shrewd, ambitious businessman who gave personal attention to all phases of his lumbering enterprises. He would be at the mill at 6 A.M., and very little in the business escaped his scrutiny.

He was devoted to his church and provided a place of worship for his workers. Schools were also a high priority. Wheeler was one of several successful lumbermen to serve in the national and state legislatures. Both he and a son, Alexander, served as leaders of the conservation movement in the Pennsylvania General Assembly.

Nathan also served as a member of the U.S. Congress.

Many Pennsylvania lumber towns had a reputation for lawlessness and heavy drinking, and respectable citizens did not feel they could venture out. This was not so at any Wheeler operation. No liquor was sold. Men and women became dependable Christians by following the example of Nathan P. Wheeler. His town was named Endeavor because of the Christian work.

Unlike Collins, Wheeler grew up in a successful lumbering family and fulfilled a legacy started by his father, which would continue for more generations, along Tionesta and Hickory Creeks. Twenty acres of Wheeler forest holdings, known as "Heart's Content," were given to the federal government and today are an important part of the Allegheny National Forest.

THE NEED FOR CONSERVATION

By 1900, the lumber industry had, in slightly more than a century, gone from up-down sawmills with a capacity of less

Depletion of the Forest. Decades of lumbering yielded many millions of feet of lumber and great profits, but also left acres of forest depleted. PENNSYLVANIA LUMBER MUSEUM

Joseph Rothrock, here with his dog Rab at Pulpit Rock in Franklin County, was an early advocate of forest conservation who made significant strides toward establishing the commonwealth's role in forestry. PENNSYLVANIA LUMBER MUSEUM

than a thousand board feet per day to mills that used a variety of saws to produce several hundred thousand feet of boards per day. The people involved could see better than anyone the depletion of the forests. Soon they would be completely harvested, but the lumbermen did not slow down. In 1906, fifty-seven mills in Pennsylvania produced more than three million board feet per year; there were hundreds more with smaller output. The three largest of these mills were in Potter County. The Goodyear Company's mill at Galeton had the highest production, with a yearly output of ninety-two million board feet. Its mill at Austin was second, with seventy-two million board feet, and the Lackawanna Company's mill at Cross Fork was third, with a yearly output of almost sixty-nine million board feet. Each of these mills was in operation for less than a decade.

For two centuries, the relentless use of Pennsylvania's forests was overlooked by most people. As long as profits were realized, the loss of the forests did not seem to matter. It would take someone with authority or influence to push for the need to conserve in order to avoid depleting the commonwealth's natural resources.

THE BUREAU OF FORESTRY

Gov. John F. Hartranft, who took office in 1873, was the first Pennsylvania governor to call attention to the need for forest legislation. The next governor, Henry M. Hoyt, discussed the future of the forests with the State Board of Agriculture and authorized a report, but nothing came of it. In 1891, during the administration of Gov. Robert E. Pattison, the first forest reserve bill was introduced, urging the creation of three state forest reservations of forty thousand acres each.

The Department of Agriculture was created in 1895, and a special Division of Forestry was organized. Just after the turn of the century, forestry was made a separate department. Within four years, the new department had almost 550,000 acres under its control. Its mission was to regenerate the forest, protect the watersheds, and extinguish forest fires.

Gifford Pinchot held forestry positions at both the state and national levels and, in Pennsylvania, helped ensure the Department of Forestry's success. He later served two terms as governor. PENNSYLVANIA LUMBER MUSEUM

When a forestry school was set up at Mont Alto, Pennsylvania finally had a facility to train foresters.

Perhaps the most tireless worker on behalf of the forests was Joseph Rothrock, who spent several years on the road in a buckboard pulled by two horses, named Dick and Bob, for the Pennsylvania Forestry Association. He carried a message about the forest problems to the people: "Forests are a crop, protect them from fire, take care of them." He did get people to understand the state's role in forestry, and for his dedication and hard work, he became known as "the Father of Pennsylvania Forestry."

In 1895, Rothrock was appointed the state's first commissioner of forestry, and he was responsible for the success of the department's early activities. By the time of its organization, the state's timberland was mostly stripped or in a brushy con-dition, and the new commission had to meet the challenge of maintaining forests as an important crop. This statement by Rothrock gives an idea of his goals: "The art of forestry is a production of the largest crop of the most desirable timber in the least time and the least expense on land that is unsuited for remunerative agriculture, or for profitable grazing." Many factors entered into the picture: the careless attitude of the people, lack of trained foresters, fire hazard because of forest conditions, and lack of money to purchase land. It would take time. Rothrock was not one to waste time, however, and he almost immediately began to build up the forest reservations. In the north-central plateau, the cut-over land was of little value to the lumbermen, so it was available at a very low cost, sometimes only a few dollars per acre. At the same time, the iron industry changed from charcoal to coal as the fuel for its furnaces, leaving some companies with thousands of acres of forestland that had little value for them. In ten years, the Pennsylvania Department of Forestry had obtained 632,000 acres, about 30 percent of the 2,000,000 acres that it owns today.

Illness forced Rothrock to retire from the commission at the age of eighty in 1904. Several ambitious and capable men—Robert Conklin, Rothrock's clerk who assumed Rothrock's duties upon his retirement; George Wirt, the first professionally trained forester in the state's service; and Gifford Pinchot, who headed the national forest service under Theodore Roosevelt and was later Pennsylvania's Commissioner of Forestry—carried on the work and guaranteed the future success of the Department of Forestry. The 1915 Act established a bureau of forest protection within the Pennsylvania Department of Forestry;

the new bureau was responsible for preventing, controlling, and extinguishing fires on all forestland. This was a tremendous assignment because of the rural population's attitude toward the forests. Many residents felt that it was more important to have a good huckleberry crop than to save trees, so they burned over forestland so that the berries would grow. Also, the few dollars unemployed residents could make fighting fires made a little arson worthwhile. New measures have improved fire control, and early detection along with today's desire to protect the environment have helped to reduce forest fires in Pennsylvania.

CIVILIAN CONSERVATION CORPS (CCC)

The presidential election of 1928 took place during a time of great affluence. Business was booming, and candidate Herbert Hoover was confident when he promised, "A chicken in every pot, and a car in every garage." Hoover won the election at a time of an economic growth never before experienced by our nation. Who would have guessed that within months the nation would face the Great Depression?

Hoover's laissez-faire policy of dealing with the economic problem was not even slightly successful. The people needed help, so the voters in the 1932 election turned to Franklin D. Roosevelt, who promised relief to an almost panicky population and easily won the presidency. FDR's plan, commonly called the New Deal, contained several work relief programs, one of which was the Civilian Conservation Corps (CCC).

In Pennsylvania and other states, the cut-over forests were in need of help, and several species of trees were in danger of extinction, including the mighty white pine. Since the country had just lost its chestnut trees, those in the Forest Service had reason for concern and were happy when Roosevelt developed a program that he felt would save the forests, provide work for young unemployed men, and help the economy.

Less than a month after FDR took office on March 20, 1933, the first CCC camp, appropriately named Camp Roosevelt, was established at Luray, Virginia. During a year of light resistance and much organization, the nation performed the greatest peacetime movement of men in its history. The speed of organization seemed miraculous, and before the end of the summer, a quarter of a million young men were enrolled in the CCC. Pennsylvania was among the leading states in the number of camps. By September 1938, eighty-eight camp sites were marked, and most were working in the state forests. There were camps in the national forests and a few on private lands. In each of the ten subdistricts in the commonwealth, there was a camp for veterans of World War I. Camps were segregated, with separate camps for African American men.

The first recruits were unmarried men between the ages of eighteen and twenty-five, from families receiving relief. Age requirements were changed later. Each enrollee would earn $30 but was given only $5 for his own use; the other $25 was sent to his family. While in camp, the men were given food, clothing, and shelter, so the $5 went far, especially in the 1930s.

The Pennsylvania Department of Forests and Waters was in charge of each subdistrict and determined the work projects, which were usually forest or stream improvement. During the nine years it was in operation, the CCC built roads, planted trees, pulled gooseberry bushes to help stop the spread of white pine blister rust, erected fire towers, fought forest fires, and opened fire trails. Several state parks, including dams and buildings that are still in use today, were created in Pennsylvania.

The CCC often answered the call for emergency service. During the winter of 1935–36, in the 3rd Corps District's tenth subdistrict, where the Lumber Museum is located, a crew from Ole Bull Camp responded to a call at Germania to shovel snow so that a funeral could be held. Another time the men removed snow for a doctor's visit. Perhaps the greatest emergency aid was given to towns and cities located along the Susquehanna and other rivers, when the men cleaned up after the St. Patrick's Day flood of 1936. That same year, an ice storm broke down many forest trees,

The Civilian Conservation Corps employed young men for projects across the nation during the Depression. Among other projects, CCC workers in Pennsylvania built trails in the forests. PENNSYLVANIA LUMBER MUSEUM

creating the need for another cleanup. A few camps had been closed in 1935, when the corps was reduced in size, and they had to be reopened for the forest cleaning emergency. Because of the necessary haste at the time of the camp openings, the sites had no permanent buildings. Tents were used for barracks and for other facilities and remained in use, sometimes into the winter. The kitchen and mess hall were one of the first to be erected, and then the five barracks were built, each with a capacity of forty enrollees. Other structures on the sites were a headquarters building used by the officers and staff, a recreation hall that often contained the camp store, and a school used for a variety of skills and classes taught by a person who officers felt was qualified. There were also medical and dental offices. As the camps were located away from electric lines, they needed generators and coal storage. These, along with latrine and bath house, made up the army's sections of the camp.

The camps were under the jurisdiction of the military, with a few officers and lesser personnel on base. Discipline was much the same as in the regular branches of the service. There was no jail, so the common punishment was extra duty or a reduction in pay. More serious cases were handled by civil authorities or by discharge from the corps.

The forestry section located nearby had blacksmith and repair shops, an office, and several storage facilities, including a garage and a quarters building. If any buildings remain at the sites today, they are often the quarters of the captain or those of the foresters. Two other features also mark the locations: a stone chimney and spruce trees.

In Potter County, Subdistrict Ten, the CCC constructed 207 miles of new

CCC Tent Camps. *While working for the CCC, men lived in temporary camps until permanent structures were built.* PENNSYLVANIA LUMBER MUSEUM

roads; built or rebuilt 800 miles of fire trails; strung 114 miles of telephone lines; cleaned up 25,000 acres of state forest after the ice storm of 1936; reduced fire hazards along trails; developed several state parks, including Cherry Springs, Ole Bull, Patterson, and Prouty; constructed Cherry Springs fire tower and the replica of the Cherry Springs Hotel; improved at least 3,000 acres of forestland; planted 1,252,300 trees; fought forest fires; improved streams; and worked to control white pine blister rust.

After World War II broke out in Europe and the American economy began to improve, ending the Depression, the need for the CCC decreased, but no legislation was enacted to end it. By the time the United States entered the war, only a few camps remained. These were closed during July 1942 after nine years of work that had successfully changed the face of parts of rural America.

MANAGING AND CONSERVING PENNSYLVANIA'S FORESTS

The prime mission of Pennsylvania's Bureau of Forestry, now part of the state's Department of Conservation and Natural Resources, is stated in the commonwealth's Constitution: "Pennsylvania's public natural resources are the common property of all of the people. As trustees of these resources the Commonwealth shall conserve and maintain them for the benefit of all the people."

The new forest in Pennsylvania today is different. The spar timber and the giant oaks and hemlocks are gone. Second- and third-growth trees are being cut. The giant pines and hemlocks were completely harvested, while many hardwoods were left to reseed and grow the present forests. With proper management, the green hills will continue to provide economic benefit as well as aesthetic enjoyment for many people for years to come.

Visiting the Site

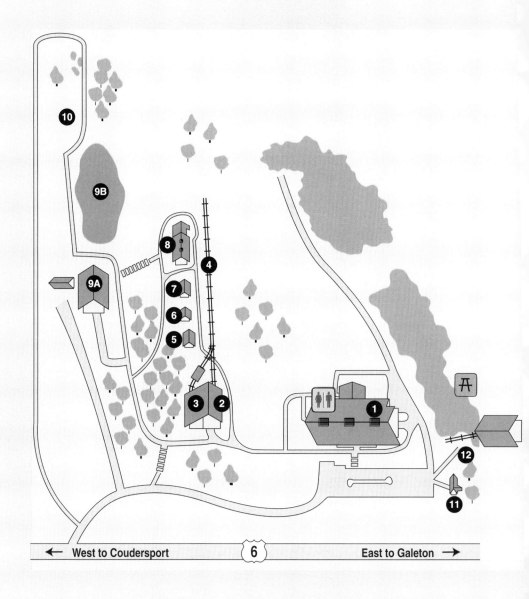

West to Coudersport ←   6   East to Galeton →

SITE LEGEND

1 Visitor Center

2 The Engine House

3 The Barnhart Model 10 Log Loader

4 Log Cars

5 The Horse Barn

6 Saw Filing Exhibit

7 The Blacksmith Shop

8 Bunkhouse and Mess Hall

9A Sawmill

9B Log Holding Pond

10 Sustainable Forestry Trail

11 CCC Chestnut Log Cabin

12 Brookville "Critter"

Restrooms

Picnic Tables

---

1 **VISITOR CENTER**

One of the most important functions of a museum is interpretation, and this begins at the Visitor Center. This and all of the other structures were built using hemlock in a board-and-batten style, which was used at many lumber camps.

Here you purchase your ticket and receive an introduction to Pennsylvania's lumber industry. In the Visitor Center are the museum offices, library, gift shop, and two large galleries with exhibits that explain some of the general history of the industry.

ART BECKER

PENNSYLVANIA LUMBER MUSEUM

The Museum's logging camp is recreated to the period 1900–1910 and represents a camp that would have been located in the hemlock forest.

2 THE ENGINE HOUSE

Few camps had a building to house an engine and other railroad equipment. A few of the largest camps had an open-end building in which the locomotive or the log loader could be worked on. Here the Engine House is the home of a Shay engine, which was acquired for the museum by the Penn-York Lumbermen's Club. This engine was the invention of a Michigan lumberman, Ephraim Shay. His invention was sold throughout the United States and in foreign countries, but nowhere was it used more than in northern Pennsylvania. More than

three hundred Shay engines were used in the commonwealth, and they played an important function in the final harvesting of the virgin forests of the northern plateau. Only a few of these behemoths of the mountains remain today.

The Shay was a geared locomotive used on steep mountain slopes. It enabled the lumbermen to cut timber that had previously been inaccessible. Two other geared locomotives, the Heisler and the Climax, were manufactured in Pennsylvania, but they were not as popular in this area as the Shay.

This engine is a seventy-ton Shay built in 1908 and delivered in 1912 to the Erbacon and Summerville Railroad in Erbacon, West Virginia. It was used by several West Virginia lumber companies before it was retired in 1954. It was moved to its present location in 1972.

3 **THE BARNHART MODEL 10 LOG LOADER**

After the first log loaders appeared in 1885, at least six different companies competed to sell their patents to the loggers. There were two types: those that operated from the main track, and those that ran on rails placed on the log cars themselves.

The Lumber Museum's log loader was designed in 1887 by Henry Barnhart, a cofounder of the Marion Power Shovel Company of Marion, Ohio. The idea for this loader is credited to Frank Goodyear, who operated in north-central Pennsylvania and harvested the timber from the site of the Lumber Museum during the early 1900s. Although this is the type of loader used in the lumber operations here, this particular machine was used in West Virginia. The only surviving Model 10, it was acquired by the Penn-York Lumbermen's Club from the Ely Thomas Lumber Company for the museum and was restored by the Pennsylvania Lumber Museum Associates (PALMA). An addition was made to the Engine House to house the loader; it was dedicated in 1997.

ART BECKER

43

4 LOG CARS

When railroads were first introduced into the lumber woods, the cars were low, with small wheels, and were loaded by large crews of men using peaveys. The use of the Barnhart Model 10 log loaders, which ran on top of the cars and added several tons, made it necessary to use higher and stronger cars. The number of logs making a load varied, depending on their size. The standard-gauge car, loaded by a loader, held about thirty-two hundred to thirty-five hundred board feet of logs.

The museum's two log cars were constructed with heavy oak timbers. Each has two pairs of four-wheeled arch-bar trucks, permanently joined by oak timbers about twenty-two feet long. The wheels are thirty-three inches in diameter. These log cars were funded and rebuilt by the museum volunteers, assisted by a matching grant from the Pennsylvania Historical and Museum Commission (PHMC).

5 THE HORSE BARN

Horses were important during a lumbering operation. They were used during the railroad era to get the logs to a landing to be loaded on the cars. During the log-driving era, when logs were floated to the booms, the teamsters used horses to pull logs to the streams to be stacked. After the drive began, they used them to return logs that had become landlocked by the splash to the stream.

The camp teamsters spent much of their spare time in the barn, grooming and caring for their horses. This barn would not have been large enough for a camp of this size, but it gives an idea of the appearance of a lumber camp's horse barn.

6 SAW FILING EXHIBIT

The care and filing of cross-cut saws was called "fitting." Some filers had a small building at the camp, but others preferred to work in a more primitive atmosphere near the cutting.

The filer was a busy man, as no sawyer wanted to work with a dull, unfitted saw. The continuous use of the saws caused them to require frequent sharpening and setting, so the person who did the fitting would do about one saw per hour, sometimes more.

Axes were usually sharpened by the woodsman himself, using a grinding wheel turned by another man.

7 THE BLACKSMITH SHOP

Wood was king, but it could not be harvested without iron or steel tools, which had to be made and repaired by the blacksmith. All tools used by the log handlers, skidders, or river drivers were used by strong men who were sometimes trying to move an almost immovable force, so tools were often bent or broken and brought back to the smithy for repair. It also was his job to see that the horses were properly shod, and in many camps, he made the horseshoes.

ART BECKER

8 BUNKHOUSE AND MESS HALL

The mess hall gives you an idea how meals were served. Meals were large and included meat, vegetables, potatoes, and dessert. The men ate in silence.

ART BECKER

ART BECKER

9 SAWMILL AND LOG HOLDING POND

The Lumber Museum's Sawmill is typical of those used by owners of small tracts or men who did contract cutting. Circular saws such as the one in this mill were not widely accepted throughout Pennsylvania until about the time of the Civil War. They have been used since then in many of the smaller mills and some larger mills, although the largest mills most often used band and gang saws. Sawmills often had a pond such as this one, where the water washed the dirt and stones from the logs. Also, soaking logs in the water softened them and made sawing easier.

PENNSYLVANIA LUMBER MUSEUM

ART BECKER

10 SUSTAINABLE FORESTRY TRAIL

This trail is a result of a joint educational project of the museum and the Pennsylvania Department of Conservation and Natural Resources Bureau of Forestry, with consultation and financial assistance provided by the Pennsylvania Hardwoods Development Council and the Sustainable Forestry Initiative of Pennsylvania. The trail explains the role of the timber harvests in sustaining forests and offers an opportunity to learn the methods of developing and keeping a healthy forest.

ART BECKER

The Trail follows along Commissioner Run northward from the roadside rest adjacent to U.S. Route 6 through an area that was cut over in three stages between 1908 and 1921. Lumber camps and a railroad spur were located near the demonstration areas. Two of the plots feature practices that encourage natural regeneration and another shows what to expect in a nonsustainable environment.